TABLE OF CONTENTS

Chapter 1

1.1 Understanding React Native's Design Philosophy
1.2 Core UI Building Blocks
1.3 Introducing Flexbox for Layout

Chapter 2

2.1 Font Families and Styling
2.2 Text Input and User Interaction
2.3 Internationalization and Localization

Chapter 3

3.1 Choosing Effective Color Palettes
3.2 Working with Gradients and Shadows
3.3 Implementing Themes and Dark Mode

Chapter 4

4.1 Creating Intuitive Navigation Flows
4.2 Customizing Transitions and Animations
4.3 Implementing Gestures for Navigation

Chapter 5

5.1 FlatList and SectionList Components
5.2 Customizing List Item Appearance
5.3 Implementing Pull-to-Refresh and Infinite Scrolling

Chapter 6

6.1 Buttons and Touchable Elements
6.2 Modals and Overlays
6.3 Progress Indicators and Loaders

Chapter 7

7.1 The Animated API
7.2 Creating Micro-interactions
7.3 Advanced Animation Techniques

Chapter 8

8.1 Detecting Platform Differences
8.2 Conditional Rendering for Platform-Specific UI
8.3 Using Native Modules for Platform-Specific Features

Chapter 9

9.1 Building Reusable UI Components
9.2 Implementing a Design System
9.3 Utilizing Popular UI Libraries

Chapter 10

10.1 Understanding Accessibility Principles
10.2 Implementing Accessibility Features
10.3 Testing for Accessibility

PREFACE

In the ever-evolving landscape of mobile development, React Native has emerged as a powerful and versatile framework for crafting truly native experiences using the familiar comfort of JavaScript. But building an app that merely functions is no longer enough. Users today expect apps that are not only performant and reliable but also beautiful, engaging, and delightful to use.

This book, "React Native: Crafting Elegant UIs for iOS and Android," is your guide to mastering the art of UI design in the React Native world. Whether you're a seasoned React Native developer looking to elevate your UI skills or a web developer venturing into the realm of mobile, this book will equip you with the knowledge and techniques to create user interfaces that are both visually stunning and functionally impeccable.

Throughout these pages, we'll embark on a journey through the core principles of UI design, exploring typography, color theory, navigation, animations, and more. We'll delve into the intricacies of React Native's component-based architecture, mastering layout with Flexbox, crafting engaging lists, and building interactive elements that respond seamlessly to user input.

But this book goes beyond the basics. We'll also explore advanced techniques for creating complex animations, implementing platform-specific adaptations, and building reusable component libraries that promote consistency and maintainability. And because accessibility is paramount, we'll dedicate a chapter to ensuring your app is usable by everyone, regardless of their abilities.

By the end of this book, you'll have the skills and confidence to craft React Native UIs that are not only visually elegant but also user-friendly, accessible, and performant. So, let's dive in and unlock the full potential of React Native to create mobile experiences that truly shine.

Chapter 1

Foundations of Elegant UI in React Native

1.1 Understanding React Native's Design Philosophy

So, you want to build a mobile app. You've got this amazing idea, a vision of how it'll look, how users will interact... but then reality hits. There's not one, but *two* major platforms to conquer: iOS and Android. Traditionally, this meant becoming a master of two completely different worlds. You'd need to learn Swift or Objective-C for iOS, Java or Kotlin for Android, wrestle with different development tools, and essentially build the same app twice. Ouch.

Enter React Native. This framework throws you a lifeline, allowing you to use your trusty JavaScript skills (and maybe a bit of React knowledge) to create truly native apps for *both* platforms. How? Through its elegant "Learn Once, Write Anywhere" philosophy.

What does that *really* mean?

Learn Once: If you're already comfortable building for the web with JavaScript and React, you're off to a great start. React Native uses the same component-based structure, JSX syntax for describing your UI, and even similar ideas for managing your app's data (we'll get to that later). This significantly lowers the barrier to entry for web developers wanting to make the leap to mobile.

Write Anywhere: Now, this doesn't mean writing *identical* code that magically works perfectly on both iOS and Android. Instead,

React Native provides a clever abstraction. You write your UI code once using React Native components, and the framework takes care of translating those components into their native equivalents. You write a `<View>` component, and React Native renders it as a `UIView` on iOS and an `android.view` on Android - behind the scenes, without you needing to worry about the platform-specific details.

This "magic" happens thanks to something called the **bridge**. Imagine it as a communication channel between your JavaScript code and the native side of each platform. Your JavaScript tells React Native what UI to build, and the bridge relays those instructions to the native platform, which then renders the actual native UI components.

Consistency: You can maintain a unified design language and user experience across platforms. Your app will feel familiar and intuitive to users whether they're on an iPhone or an Android device.

Efficiency: React Native enables rapid prototyping and iteration. You can quickly test your UI ideas on both platforms, saving valuable time and effort.

Focus on Design: By abstracting away many platform-specific details, React Native frees you to focus on what you do best: crafting beautiful, functional, and engaging user interfaces.

With this foundational understanding, we're ready to dive into the core UI building blocks that will empower you to bring your app designs to life. Let's begin!

1.2 Core UI Building Blocks

(Views, Text, Images, and their styling properties)

Alright, we've got the big-picture philosophy down. Now, let's get our hands dirty with the actual building blocks of any React Native UI. Think of these as your raw materials, the Lego bricks you'll use to assemble beautiful and functional interfaces.

Views: The Foundation

In React Native, almost everything you see on the screen is, at its core, a `View`. It's the most fundamental UI component, a rectangular container that holds and arranges other elements. Think of it like a `div` in web development, but with superpowers.

Here's a simple example:

JavaScript

```javascript
import React from 'react';
import { View, Text } from 'react-native';

const MyComponent = () => {
  return (
    <View>
      <Text>Hello, world!</Text>
    </View>
  );
};
```

This code snippet renders a `View` that contains a `Text` component displaying "Hello, world!". Simple, right? But don't be fooled by its simplicity. `View`s are incredibly versatile. You can nest them within each other to create complex layouts, and you can style them to control their size, position, background color, borders, and much more.

Text: Communicating with Users

The `Text` component is your primary tool for displaying text in your app. Whether it's headings, paragraphs, labels, or buttons, `Text` handles it all.

JavaScript

```
<Text style={{ fontSize: 24, fontWeight: 'bold' }}>
  This is a heading
</Text>
<Text>
  This is a paragraph of text. You can customize its font, color, line height, and more.
</Text>
```

Images: Adding Visual Appeal

No app is complete without images. The `Image` component lets you display images from various sources, including local files, network URLs, and even data URIs.

JavaScript

```
<Image
  source={{ uri: 'https://example.com/my-image.jpg' }}
  style={{ width: 200, height: 200 }}
/>
```

Styling with StyleSheets

Now, how do you make these building blocks look good? That's where styling comes in. React Native provides a `StyleSheet` API that lets you define styles in a way that's familiar to web developers, using JavaScript objects.

JavaScript

```javascript
import { StyleSheet } from 'react-native';

const styles = StyleSheet.create({
  container: {
    flex: 1,
    backgroundColor: '#fff',
    alignItems: 'center',
    justifyContent: 'center',[1]
  },
  heading: {
    fontSize: 32,
    fontWeight: 'bold',[2]
    color: '#007bff',
  },
});
```

You can then apply these styles to your components:

JavaScript

```javascript
<View style={styles.container}>
  <Text style={styles.heading}>Welcome!</Text>
</View>
```

Flexbox: Mastering Layout

Flexbox is a powerful layout system that gives you fine-grained control over how your components are arranged within a `View`. It's essential for creating responsive and dynamic UIs that adapt to different screen sizes and orientations.

Beyond the Basics

These are just the foundational building blocks. React Native offers a rich set of built-in components and APIs for creating more complex UI elements like buttons, lists, and forms. We'll explore those in the upcoming chapters.

But for now, get comfortable with `View`, `Text`, `Image`, and `StyleSheet`. They're the core ingredients you'll use to craft every UI in your React Native journey.

1.3 Introducing Flexbox for Layout

(Mastering the flexible box model for dynamic layouts)

Alright, you've got your `View`s, `Text`, and `Image`s ready. Now, how do you arrange them on the screen in a way that looks good and adapts to different screen sizes? That's where Flexbox comes in.

Think of Flexbox as a super-powered layout system that gives you incredible control over the arrangement of your components. It's like having a magic wand that can align, distribute, and resize your UI elements with ease.

The Core Concepts

Flexbox revolves around two main axes:

Main Axis: This is the primary direction in which your components are laid out. It can be either horizontal (row) or vertical (column).

Cross Axis: This is the perpendicular direction to the main axis.

Imagine a row of books on a shelf. The shelf is the main axis, and the height of the shelf is the cross axis.

Key Flexbox Properties

Here are some of the most important Flexbox properties you'll use in React Native:

`flexDirection`: This determines the direction of the main axis. `row` arranges items horizontally, while `column` arranges them vertically.

`justifyContent`: This controls how items are aligned along the main axis. You can use values like `flex-start` (align to the start), `center` (align to the center), `flex-end` (align to the end), `space-around` (distribute space around items), and `space-between` (distribute space between items).

`alignItems`: This controls how items are aligned along the cross axis. You can use similar values as `justifyContent`, such as `flex-start`, `center`, `flex-end`, and `stretch` (stretch items to fill the container).

`flex`: This property allows you to control how much space an item takes up within its container. You can assign numeric values to indicate the relative size of items.

Flexbox in Action

Let's see an example. Say you want to create a simple layout with three buttons arranged horizontally, centered both horizontally and vertically on the screen:

JavaScript

```javascript
import React from 'react';
import { View, Button, StyleSheet } from 'react-native';

const MyComponent = () => {
  return (
    <View style={styles.container}>
      <Button title="Button 1" />
      <Button title="Button 2" />
      <Button title="Button 3" />
    </View>
  );
};

const styles = StyleSheet.create({
  container: {
    flex: 1,
    flexDirection: 'row',
    alignItems: 'center',
    justifyContent: 'center',
  },
});
```

In this example, `flexDirection: 'row'` arranges the buttons horizontally. `alignItems: 'center'` centers them vertically, and `justifyContent: 'center'` centers them horizontally.

Dynamic Layouts

The real power of Flexbox lies in its ability to create dynamic layouts that adapt to different screen sizes and orientations. By combining Flexbox properties and understanding how they interact, you can create UIs that look great on any device.

Mastering Flexbox

Flexbox can seem a bit daunting at first, but with practice and experimentation, you'll quickly grasp its core concepts and unlock its full potential. Don't be afraid to play around with different properties and see how they affect your layout.

As you become more comfortable with Flexbox, you'll be able to create complex and responsive UIs with ease, ensuring your app looks fantastic on any device.

Chapter 2

Typography and Text Handling

2.1 Font Families and Styling

(Exploring system fonts, custom fonts, and font properties)

Typography is the art and technique of arranging type to make written language legible, readable, and appealing.[1] In the realm of mobile UI design, it plays a crucial role in creating a visually engaging and user-friendly experience.[2]

React Native provides a robust set of tools for controlling the appearance of text in your app, allowing you to craft elegant and effective typography.

System Fonts: A Reliable Foundation

Every mobile platform comes with a set of pre-installed fonts, known as system fonts.[3] These fonts are designed to be highly legible and optimized for the platform's aesthetics.[4]

In React Native, you can easily access and utilize these system fonts. Here's an example:

JavaScript

```
<Text style={{ fontFamily: 'System' }}>This text uses the system font.</Text>
```

On iOS, this will typically render as San Francisco, while on Android, it will use Roboto. Using system fonts ensures your app blends seamlessly with the platform's overall design language.[5]

Custom Fonts: Adding Personality

While system fonts provide a solid foundation, you might want to add a unique touch to your app's typography by using custom fonts. These fonts can help you establish a distinct brand identity or create a specific visual style.[6]

To use a custom font in React Native, you'll first need to add it to your project's assets and then link it in your styles.[7]

(This section would benefit from a step-by-step guide on how to add and link custom fonts in a React Native project.)

Font Properties: Fine-tuning the Appearance

React Native offers a wide range of font properties that allow you to fine-tune the appearance of your text. These properties include:

`fontSize`: Controls the size of the font.[8]

`fontWeight`: Specifies the weight of the font, such as `normal`, `bold`, or numeric values like `100`, `400`, `700`.

`fontStyle`: Sets the style of the font to `normal` or `italic`.

`color`: Determines the color of the text.[9]

`lineHeight`: Controls the spacing between lines of text.[10]

`letterSpacing`: Adjusts the spacing between letters.[11]

`textAlign`: Aligns the text to the `left`, `center`, or `right`.

Here's an example of how to use these properties:

JavaScript

```
<Text style={{
  fontFamily: 'CustomFont',
  fontSize: 24,
  fontWeight: 'bold',
  color: '#e91e63',
  textAlign: 'center'
}}>
    This text uses a custom font and various styling properties.
</Text>
```

Beyond the Basics

In addition to these basic properties, React Native provides more advanced features for text styling, such as:

Text Decoration: Adding underlines, overlines, and strikethroughs.

Text Shadow: Creating subtle shadow effects for text.

Text Transform: Transforming text to uppercase, lowercase, or capitalize.

By mastering these font families and styling properties, you'll be well-equipped to create beautiful and effective typography that enhances the overall user experience of your React Native app.

2.2 Text Input and User Interaction

(Crafting user-friendly forms and input fields)

While displaying text effectively is crucial, many apps also require users to *input* text. Whether it's filling out forms, composing messages, or searching for information, providing a smooth and intuitive text input experience is essential for a positive user experience.

The `TextInput` Component

React Native's `TextInput` component is your gateway to capturing user input. It renders a text field where users can type in information. Here's a basic example:

JavaScript

```
import React, { useState } from 'react';
import { TextInput, View, Text } from 'react-native';

const MyComponent = () => {
  const [text, setText] = useState('');

  return (
    <View>
      <TextInput
        style={{ height: 40, borderColor: 'gray', borderWidth: 1 }}
        onChangeText={setText}
        value={text}
        placeholder="Enter your name"
      />
      <Text>Hello, {text}!</Text>
    </View>
```

```
    );
};
```

This code snippet renders a text input field with a placeholder. As the user types, the `onChangeText` prop updates the `text` state, which is then displayed in the `Text` component below.

Key Properties and Customization

`TextInput` offers a wealth of properties to customize its appearance and behavior:

`placeholder`: Displays placeholder text when the input is empty.

`value`: Controls the current value of the input field.

`secureTextEntry`: Masks the input for sensitive data like passwords.

`keyboardType`: Sets the keyboard type (e.g., `email-address`, `numeric`).

`multiline`: Allows for multiline text input.

`maxLength`: Limits the number of characters.

`onSubmitEditing`: Triggers an action when the user submits the input (e.g., by pressing Enter).

Crafting User-Friendly Forms

Text input fields are often used within forms. To create user-friendly forms, consider these best practices:

Clear Labels: Provide descriptive labels for each input field.

Visual Feedback: Indicate when a field is focused or has an error.

Input Validation: Validate user input to ensure data integrity.

Error Handling: Display helpful error messages to guide users.

Accessibility: Ensure your forms are accessible to users with disabilities (e.g., using appropriate ARIA attributes).

Enhancing User Interaction

Beyond basic text input, you can enhance user interaction with features like:

Autocorrect: Enable or disable autocorrection.

Autocomplete: Suggest possible completions for the input.

Keyboard Handling: Control keyboard behavior (e.g., showing/hiding the keyboard).

By mastering the `TextInput` component and following best practices for form design, you can create intuitive and user-friendly input experiences that enhance the overall usability of your React Native app.

2.3 Internationalization and Localization

(Adapting your UI for different languages)

In today's interconnected world, your app might be used by people from all corners of the globe, speaking various languages and having diverse cultural expectations. To create a truly welcoming and inclusive experience, your app needs to adapt to these

Crafting User-Friendly Forms

Text input fields are often used within forms. To create user-friendly forms, consider these best practices:

Clear Labels: Provide descriptive labels for each input field.

Visual Feedback: Indicate when a field is focused or has an error.

Input Validation: Validate user input to ensure data integrity.

Error Handling: Display helpful error messages to guide users.

Accessibility: Ensure your forms are accessible to users with disabilities (e.g., using appropriate ARIA attributes).

Enhancing User Interaction

Beyond basic text input, you can enhance user interaction with features like:

Autocorrect: Enable or disable autocorrection.

Autocomplete: Suggest possible completions for the input.

Keyboard Handling: Control keyboard behavior (e.g., showing/hiding the keyboard).

By mastering the `TextInput` component and following best practices for form design, you can create intuitive and user-friendly input experiences that enhance the overall usability of your React Native app.

2.3 Internationalization and Localization

(Adapting your UI for different languages)

In today's interconnected world, your app might be used by people from all corners of the globe, speaking various languages and having diverse cultural expectations. To create a truly welcoming and inclusive experience, your app needs to adapt to these

```
    );
};
```

This code snippet renders a text input field with a placeholder. As the user types, the `onChangeText` prop updates the `text` state, which is then displayed in the `Text` component below.

Key Properties and Customization

`TextInput` offers a wealth of properties to customize its appearance and behavior:

`placeholder`: Displays placeholder text when the input is empty.

`value`: Controls the current value of the input field.

`secureTextEntry`: Masks the input for sensitive data like passwords.

`keyboardType`: Sets the keyboard type (e.g., `email-address`, `numeric`).

`multiline`: Allows for multiline text input.

`maxLength`: Limits the number of characters.

`onSubmitEditing`: Triggers an action when the user submits the input (e.g., by pressing Enter).

different languages and cultures. This is where internationalization and localization come into play.

Internationalization (i18n): Laying the Groundwork

Internationalization, often abbreviated as i18n, is the process of designing and developing your app in a way that makes it adaptable to various languages and regions without requiring engineering changes. It's about creating a foundation that allows for easy localization.

Here are key considerations for internationalization in React Native:

Text Handling: Avoid hardcoding text directly in your components. Instead, use a separate translation file or service that stores text in different languages.

Dates, Times, and Numbers: Use libraries like `Intl` or `moment` to format dates, times, and numbers according to the user's locale.

Layout Flexibility: Design your UI with flexibility in mind, as translated text might take up more or less space than the original.

Images and Icons: Ensure images and icons are culturally appropriate and avoid using text embedded within them.

Localization (l10n): Tailoring to Specific Cultures

Localization, often abbreviated as l10n, is the process of adapting your internationalized app for a specific target market. This involves translating text, incorporating cultural nuances, and adjusting other elements to suit the preferences of that region.

Here's how you can approach localization in React Native:

Translation Management: Use a translation management system or service to organize and manage translations for different languages.

Locale-Specific Components: Create separate components or variations for specific locales if needed.

Testing and QA: Thoroughly test your localized app to ensure accuracy and cultural appropriateness.

Libraries and Tools

React Native offers several libraries and tools to simplify internationalization and localization:

`react-intl`: A comprehensive library for formatting dates, numbers, and strings, and managing translations.

`i18n-js`: A lightweight library for handling translations.

`react-native-localize`: Provides access to device locale information.

Best Practices

Plan for i18n from the start: It's much easier to incorporate internationalization from the beginning of your project than to add it later.

Use a consistent terminology: Maintain a glossary of terms to ensure consistency across translations.

Involve native speakers: Engage native speakers for translation and cultural consultation.

By embracing internationalization and localization, you can create an app that truly connects with users worldwide, providing a personalized and culturally relevant experience that fosters inclusivity and expands your app's reach.

Chapter 3

Color Theory and Branding

3.1 Choosing Effective Color Palettes

(Understanding color harmony, accessibility, and branding)

Color is a powerful tool in UI design. It can evoke emotions, guide attention, and convey meaning. Choosing an effective color palette is crucial for creating an app that is both visually appealing and user-friendly.

Color Harmony: Creating a Balanced Look

Color harmony refers to the arrangement of colors in a way that is pleasing to the eye. There are several approaches to achieving color harmony:

Complementary Colors: Colors that are opposite each other on the color wheel (e.g., red and green, blue and orange). They create a high-contrast and vibrant look.

Analogous Colors: Colors that are adjacent to each other on the color wheel (e.g., blue, blue-green, green). They create a sense of harmony and unity.

Triadic Colors: Three colors that are evenly spaced on the color wheel (e.g., red, yellow, blue). They offer a balanced and visually interesting palette.

Monochromatic Colors: Different shades, tints, and tones of a single color. They create a subtle and sophisticated look.

Accessibility: Designing for Everyone

When choosing colors, it's essential to consider accessibility for users with visual impairments. Here are some key guidelines:

Color Contrast: Ensure sufficient contrast between text and background colors. Use tools like WebAIM's Color Contrast Checker to verify accessibility.

Color Blindness: Be mindful of color combinations that might be difficult to distinguish for people with color blindness. Use simulators to test your UI for different types of color blindness.

Avoid Color as the Sole Indicator: Don't rely solely on color to convey information. Use other visual cues like icons or patterns.

Branding: Reflecting Your Identity

Your app's color palette should align with your brand identity. Consider the emotions and messages you want to convey.

Primary Color: This is the dominant color that represents your brand.

Secondary Colors: These complement the primary color and provide variety.

Accent Colors: These are used sparingly to highlight specific elements.

Tools and Resources

Several tools and resources can assist you in choosing effective color palettes:

Adobe Color: A web-based tool for exploring and creating color palettes.

Coolors: A color palette generator that provides harmonious color combinations.

Material Design Color Tool: Helps you create color palettes that align with Material Design guidelines.

Testing and Iteration

Don't be afraid to experiment with different color palettes and gather feedback from users. Test your colors on different devices and in various lighting conditions to ensure they look their best.

By understanding color harmony, accessibility, and branding, you can create a color palette that is visually appealing, inclusive, and effectively communicates your app's identity.

3.2 Working with Gradients and Shadows

(Adding depth and visual interest to your UI)

While flat design has been popular for a while, adding subtle depth and dimension to your UI can create a more engaging and visually appealing experience. Gradients and shadows are powerful tools for achieving this effect in React Native.

Gradients: Blending Colors Smoothly

Gradients allow you to transition between two or more colors, creating a smooth and visually interesting effect. React Native provides the `LinearGradient` and `RadialGradient` components from the `expo-linear-gradient` library (you'll need to install it first) to create these effects.

`LinearGradient`: Creates a linear gradient that transitions between colors along a straight line. You can control the direction of the gradient using the `start` and `end` props.

JavaScript

```javascript
import { LinearGradient } from 'expo-linear-gradient';

<LinearGradient
  colors={['#e91e63', '#00bcd4']}
  start={{ x: 0, y: 0 }}
  end={{ x: 1, y: 1 }}
  style={{ ... }}
>
  {/* Your content here */}
</LinearGradient>
```

RadialGradient: **Creates a radial gradient that transitions between colors outwards from a central point. You can control the center, radius, and color stops.**

JavaScript

```javascript
import { RadialGradient } from 'expo-linear-gradient';

<RadialGradient
  colors={['#fff', '#000']}
  center={centerPoint}
  radius={100}
  style={{ ... }}
>
  {/* Your content here */}
</RadialGradient>
```

Shadows: Adding Depth and Realism

Shadows give your UI elements a sense of depth and realism by simulating the effect of light and shadow. You can control the appearance of shadows using the following properties in your styles:

`shadowColor`: The color of the shadow.

`shadowOffset`: The offset of the shadow from the component, with `width` and `height` properties.

`shadowOpacity`: The opacity of the shadow.

`shadowRadius`: The blur radius of the shadow.

`elevation`: (Android only) A platform-specific way to control shadow appearance.

JavaScript

```
<View style={{
  backgroundColor: '#fff',
  shadowColor: '#000',
  shadowOffset: { width: 0, height: 2 },
  shadowOpacity: 0.2,
  shadowRadius: 4,
  elevation: 5,
}}>
  {/* Your content here */}
</View>
```

Using Gradients and Shadows Effectively

Subtlety is Key: Use gradients and shadows sparingly to avoid overwhelming your UI. Subtle effects often create the most elegant look.

Visual Hierarchy: Use gradients and shadows to guide the user's attention and create visual hierarchy.

Performance Considerations: Be mindful that excessive use of shadows can impact performance, especially on older devices.

Examples and Inspiration

Show examples of how gradients and shadows can be used effectively in UI design. Consider showcasing:

Buttons with gradient backgrounds.

Cards with subtle shadows.

Progress bars with gradient fills.

By mastering gradients and shadows, you can add depth, dimension, and visual interest to your React Native UIs, creating a more engaging and polished user experience.

3.3 Implementing Themes and Dark Mode

(Creating adaptable and user-preferred color schemes)

Modern apps often offer users the ability to personalize their experience by choosing between different themes, including the increasingly popular dark mode. Implementing themes and dark mode in your React Native app not only enhances user satisfaction but also improves accessibility and can even reduce battery consumption on certain devices.

Tab Navigation: Organizing Sections

Tab navigation provides a tab bar, usually at the bottom of the screen, allowing users to quickly switch between different sections or features of your app. This is ideal for apps with distinct content categories.

Use Cases:

Social media apps with sections for home, notifications, and profile.

E-commerce apps with tabs for categories, cart, and account.

Music apps with sections for artists, albums, and playlists.

Drawer Navigation: Hidden Options

Drawer navigation provides a slide-out "drawer" that contains links to different screens or features. This is useful for providing access to secondary or less frequently used options without cluttering the main interface.

Use Cases:

Settings and preferences.

Help and support.

About the app information.

Combining Navigation Patterns

React Navigation allows you to combine these patterns to create complex navigation flows. For example, you could have a tab navigator with each tab containing a stack navigator for hierarchical content within that section.

Best Practices for Intuitive Navigation

Clear Structure: Organize your app's navigation in a logical and predictable way.

Visual Cues: Use icons, labels, and visual indicators to clearly communicate the current location and navigation options.

Back Navigation: Ensure consistent and reliable back navigation behavior.

Accessibility: Make your navigation accessible to users with disabilities (e.g., keyboard navigation).

Beyond the Basics

React Navigation offers more advanced features, such as:

Custom Transitions: Create unique transitions between screens.

Deep Linking: Allow users to access specific screens directly from external links.

Navigation State: Access and manipulate the navigation state for dynamic behavior.

By mastering these navigation patterns and following best practices, you can create intuitive and user-friendly navigation flows that enhance the overall experience of your React Native app.

4.2 Customizing Transitions and Animations

(Enhancing user experience with smooth transitions)

While React Navigation provides default transitions for navigating between screens, customizing these transitions can significantly enhance the user experience. Smooth and well-designed transitions can make your app feel more polished, responsive, and engaging.

Understanding Transitions

Transitions in React Navigation refer to the visual effects that occur when moving between screens. These effects can involve changes in opacity, position, scale, or other visual properties.

Customizing Transitions with `screenOptions`

React Navigation allows you to customize transitions using the `screenOptions` prop within your navigator. You can define transition properties like duration, easing functions, and animation styles.

JavaScript

```
<Stack.Navigator
  screenOptions={{
    transitionSpec: {
      open: config,
      close: config,
    },
                              cardStyleInterpolator: CardStyleInterpolators.forHorizontalIOS,
  }}
>
  {/* Your screens here */}
</Stack.Navigator>
```

Types of Transitions

You can create various transition effects, such as:

Fade In/Out: Smoothly fade screens in and out.

Slide In/Out: Slide screens in from different directions (left, right, top, bottom).

Scale: Scale screens up or down.

Combined Transitions: Combine multiple effects for more complex transitions.

Animation Libraries

For more advanced animations, you can leverage animation libraries like:

React Native's `Animated` **API**: Provides a powerful and flexible way to create custom animations.

`react-native-reanimated`: Offers high-performance animations that run on the native thread.

`lottie-react-native`: Allows you to integrate animations created in Adobe After Effects.

Best Practices

Keep it Subtle: Avoid overly flashy or distracting transitions. Subtle animations are often more effective.

Maintain Consistency: Use consistent transition styles throughout your app to create a cohesive experience.

Performance Considerations: Be mindful of performance, especially on lower-end devices. Optimize animations to avoid jank or lag.

Accessibility: Ensure transitions don't cause issues for users with motion sensitivities or visual impairments. Provide options to disable animations if needed.

Examples and Inspiration

Show examples of effective transitions in popular apps. Consider showcasing:

Shared element transitions, where elements seamlessly move between screens.

Card-based transitions, where screens slide in and out like cards.

Hero animations, where elements expand or contract to transition between screens.

By mastering transition customization and animation techniques, you can create a more dynamic and engaging user experience in your React Native app. Smooth and well-designed transitions can add a touch of polish and delight to your app's navigation.

4.3 Implementing Gestures for Navigation

(Swipe, pinch, and other interactive gestures)

Touchscreen devices have revolutionized how we interact with technology. Gestures like swiping, pinching, and tapping have become second nature to mobile users. Incorporating these gestures into your React Native app's navigation can create a more intuitive, engaging, and even delightful user experience.

Why Gesture-Based Navigation?

Intuitiveness: Gestures often feel more natural and intuitive than traditional buttons or menus. Swiping to go back, pinching to zoom, or tapping to select, all mimic real-world interactions.

Efficiency: Gestures can streamline navigation, allowing users to quickly access different sections or perform actions with minimal effort.

Engagement: Interactive gestures can make your app feel more dynamic and playful, increasing user engagement and satisfaction.

Implementing Gestures with React Native

React Native provides a powerful `Gesture Responder System` that allows you to detect and respond to various touch gestures.

You can use this system to implement custom gesture-based navigation.

Here's a simplified example of how to implement a swipe-to-go-back gesture:

JavaScript

```javascript
import React, { useRef } from 'react';
import { Animated, View } from 'react-native';
import { useNavigation } from '@react-navigation/native';

const MyScreen = () => {
  const navigation = useNavigation();
  const translateX = useRef(new Animated.Value(0)).current;

  const handleSwipe = ({ nativeEvent }) => {
    if (nativeEvent.translationX < -50) { // Swipe left threshold
      Animated.timing(translateX, {
        toValue: -screenWidth, // Slide screen out
        duration: 300,
        useNativeDriver: true,
      }).start(() => navigation.goBack());
    }
  };

  return (
    <Animated.View
      style={{ transform: [{ translateX }] }}
      onHorizontalDrag={handleSwipe}
    >
      {/* Your screen content here */}
```

```
        </Animated.View>
    );
};
```

This example uses the `Animated` API to create a smooth sliding animation when the user swipes left.

Common Gestures for Navigation

Swipe: Swiping left or right can be used for navigating between screens, similar to iOS's back gesture.

Pinch: Pinching in or out can be used for zooming in and out of content, particularly useful in maps or image galleries.

Long Press: A long press can be used to trigger contextual menus or actions.

Third-Party Libraries

Several third-party libraries can simplify gesture implementation:

`react-native-gesture-handler`: Provides a declarative API for handling gestures, making it easier to integrate with React Navigation.

`react-native-swipe-gestures`: Offers ready-to-use components for swipe gestures.

Best Practices

Clarity and Consistency: Use gestures in a way that is consistent with platform conventions and user expectations.

Visual Feedback: Provide visual cues to indicate that a gesture is recognized and what action it will trigger.

Accessibility: Ensure gestures are accessible to users with motor impairments. Provide alternative navigation methods.

Examples and Inspiration

Showcase examples of effective gesture-based navigation in popular apps:

Tinder's swipe-based interactions.

Instagram's double-tap to like.

Mobile game controls using gestures.

By incorporating gestures into your React Native app's navigation, you can create a more intuitive, efficient, and engaging user experience. Well-designed gestures can make your app feel more responsive and modern, enhancing user satisfaction and delight.

Chapter 5

Crafting Engaging Lists and Grids

5.1 `FlatList` and `SectionList` Components

(Efficiently rendering large lists of data)

Lists are a ubiquitous UI element in mobile apps. From displaying contacts and messages to showcasing products and news feeds, lists are essential for presenting collections of data. However, rendering large lists efficiently can be a challenge, especially on mobile devices with limited resources.

React Native provides two powerful components, `FlatList` and `SectionList`, specifically designed to handle large lists of data with optimal performance and smooth scrolling.

`FlatList`: **Your Go-To List Component**

`FlatList` is a performant and versatile component for rendering simple, scrollable lists. It's perfect for scenarios where you have a long, homogeneous list of items that don't require grouping or categorization.

Here's a basic example of how to use `FlatList`:

JavaScript

```
import React from 'react';
import { FlatList, StyleSheet, Text, View } from 'react-native';
```

```
const DATA = [
  { id: '1', title: 'Item 1' },
  { id: '2', title: 'Item 2' },
  // ... more items
];

const Item = ({ title }) => (
  <View style={styles.item}>
    <Text style={styles.title}>{title}</Text>
  </View>
);

const MyComponent = () => {
  return (
    <FlatList
      data={DATA}
          renderItem={({ item }) => <Item title={item.title} />}
      keyExtractor={item => item.id}
    />
  );
```

```
};


const styles = StyleSheet.create({
  // ... styles for item and title
});
```

In this example, `FlatList` takes an array of `DATA` and renders each item using the `renderItem` function. The `keyExtractor` function provides a unique key for each item, which is essential for efficient rendering and updates.

`SectionList`: **Grouping and Categorizing Data**

`SectionList` is similar to `FlatList`, but it provides additional functionality for grouping your list items into sections with headers and footers. This is ideal for scenarios where your data has a natural categorization, such as contacts grouped by alphabet or products categorized by type.

JavaScript

```
import React from 'react';

import { SectionList, StyleSheet, Text, View } from 'react-native';


const DATA = [
  {
    title: 'Section 1',
```

```
    data: [{ id: '1', title: 'Item 1' }, { id: '2', title: 'Item 2' }],
  },
  {
    title: 'Section 2',
    data: [{ id: '3', title: 'Item 3' }, { id: '4', title: 'Item 4' }],
  },
  // ... more sections
];


const Item = ({ title }) => (
  <View style={styles.item}>
    <Text style={styles.title}>{title}</Text>
  </View>
);


const MyComponent = () => {
  return (
    <SectionList
      sections={DATA}
```

```
      keyExtractor={(item, index) => item + index}
      renderItem={({ item }) => <Item title={item.title} />}
      renderSectionHeader={({ section: { title } }) => (
        <Text style={styles.header}>{title}</Text>
      )}
    />
  );
};

const styles = StyleSheet.create({
  // ... styles for item, title, and header
});
```

In this example, `SectionList` takes an array of `DATA` with sections and renders each section with a header and its corresponding items.

Benefits of `FlatList` and `SectionList`

Performance: They render only the items that are currently visible on the screen, optimizing memory usage and improving scrolling performance.

Flexibility: They provide various props for customization, such as headers, footers, separators, and pull-to-refresh functionality.

Simplicity: They offer a straightforward API for rendering lists, making it easy to manage and update your data.

By mastering `FlatList` and `SectionList`, you can efficiently render large lists of data in your React Native app, ensuring a smooth and responsive user experience even with extensive datasets.

5.2 Customizing List Item Appearance

(Designing visually appealing and informative list items)

While `FlatList` and `SectionList` provide the foundation for efficient list rendering, the real magic lies in how you design and customize the appearance of individual list items. Visually appealing and informative list items are crucial for engaging users and presenting data effectively.

The `renderItem` Function: Your Creative Canvas

The `renderItem` function is where you define the structure and style of each item in your list. This is your opportunity to get creative and tailor the appearance to suit your app's design and the specific data you're displaying.

Key Considerations for List Item Design

Content Hierarchy: Establish a clear visual hierarchy within each list item. Use typography, spacing, and color to emphasize the most important information.

Visual Appeal: Make your list items visually engaging with appropriate imagery, icons, and color accents.

Information Density: Balance the amount of information displayed in each item. Avoid overwhelming users with too much text or visual clutter.

Interaction: Consider how users will interact with list items. Will they be tappable, swipeable, or expandable?

Styling Techniques

Layout: Use Flexbox to arrange elements within each list item. Create layouts that adapt well to different screen sizes and orientations.

Typography: Choose appropriate font sizes, weights, and styles to create a clear and readable hierarchy of information.

Color: Use color strategically to highlight key information, create visual interest, and reinforce your brand identity.

Spacing: Use margins and padding to create visual breathing room and separate elements within each item.

Dividers: Use separators to visually distinguish between list items and improve readability.

Examples and Inspiration

Showcase various examples of list item designs, such as:

E-commerce product listings: Display product images, names, prices, and ratings in an attractive and informative way.

Social media feeds: Show user avatars, names, post content, and timestamps in a visually engaging format.

Messaging apps: Present messages with clear sender identification, timestamps, and message previews.

Advanced Customization

Conditional Rendering: Render different elements or styles based on the data or context of each item.

Custom Components: Create reusable components for specific types of list items.

Animations: Add subtle animations to list items to enhance interactions and visual feedback.

By mastering the art of customizing list item appearance, you can transform ordinary lists into engaging and informative displays of data. Well-designed list items contribute significantly to a positive user experience, making your React Native app more visually appealing and user-friendly.

5.3 Implementing Pull-to-Refresh and Infinite Scrolling

(Enhancing user interaction with lists)

While basic lists are functional, adding interactive elements like pull-to-refresh and infinite scrolling can significantly enhance the user experience. These features provide a more dynamic and engaging way for users to interact with your app's data.

Pull-to-Refresh: Updating Data with a Gesture

Pull-to-refresh allows users to refresh the list's content by pulling down on the list. This is a common pattern in many apps, particularly those that display frequently updated data like news feeds or social media streams.

Implementing Pull-to-Refresh with `FlatList` and `SectionList`

Both `FlatList` and `SectionList` have built-in support for pull-to-refresh. You can enable this feature using the `onRefresh` prop and the `refreshing` prop.

`onRefresh`: A function that's called when the user pulls down to refresh. This function should typically fetch new data and update the list's data source.

`refreshing`: A boolean value that indicates whether the list is currently refreshing. This is used to display a loading indicator while new data is being fetched.

JavaScript

```
<FlatList
  data={data}
  renderItem={renderItem}
  keyExtractor={keyExtractor}
  onRefresh={fetchData}
  refreshing={isLoading}
/>
```

Infinite Scrolling: Loading More Data as You Scroll

Infinite scrolling allows users to load more data as they scroll towards the end of the list. This is useful for displaying large datasets without overwhelming the user with a massive initial load.

Implementing Infinite Scrolling

You can implement infinite scrolling by:

Detecting when the user reaches the end of the list.

Fetching more data from your data source.

Appending the new data to the existing list.

`FlatList` provides the `onEndReached` prop, which is called when the user scrolls near the end of the list. You can use this prop to trigger the fetching of more data.

JavaScript

```
<FlatList
  data={data}
  renderItem={renderItem}
  keyExtractor={keyExtractor}
  onEndReached={fetchMoreData}
  onEndReachedThreshold={0.5} // Trigger when 50% from the end
/>
```

Best Practices

Visual Feedback: Provide clear visual cues to indicate that pull-to-refresh or infinite scrolling is in progress. Use loading indicators or animations to keep users informed.

Error Handling: Handle errors gracefully, such as network issues or data fetching failures. Display informative error messages and allow users to retry.

Performance Optimization: Optimize data fetching and rendering to ensure smooth scrolling and avoid performance issues.

Examples and Inspiration

Show examples of apps that implement pull-to-refresh and infinite scrolling effectively:

Twitter's infinite scrolling feed.

Gmail's pull-to-refresh for new emails.

Instagram's infinite scrolling photo feed.

By implementing pull-to-refresh and infinite scrolling, you can enhance the user experience of your React Native app, making lists more interactive, dynamic, and engaging. These features provide a seamless way for users to access and interact with large amounts of data, improving the overall usability and satisfaction of your app.

Chapter 6

Building Interactive Components

6.1 Buttons and Touchable Elements

(Designing various button styles and interactions)

Buttons are the primary way users interact with your app. They trigger actions, navigate between screens, and provide feedback. Designing effective buttons is crucial for creating a user-friendly and engaging experience. React Native offers a variety of components and APIs for creating buttons with different styles and interactions.

Core Touchable Components

React Native provides several core components for creating touchable elements:

`TouchableOpacity`: Reduces the opacity of the button when pressed, providing visual feedback.

`TouchableHighlight`: Highlights the button with a temporary background color when pressed.

`TouchableWithoutFeedback`: Doesn't provide any visual feedback, but still detects touches.

`Pressable`: A more modern and versatile component that combines the features of the other touchable components. It offers greater control over press states and visual feedback.

Button Component

While you can create custom buttons using the touchable components, React Native also provides a dedicated `Button` component that offers a basic button with platform-specific styling.

JavaScript

```
import { Button } from 'react-native';
```

```
<Button title="Press me" onPress={() => alert('Button pressed!')} />
```

Designing Button Styles

You can customize the appearance of your buttons using various styling properties:

`backgroundColor`: Sets the background color of the button.

`color`: Sets the text color of the button.

`fontSize`: Controls the font size of the button text.

`padding`: Adds padding around the button content.

`borderRadius`: Rounds the corners of the button.

`borderWidth` **and** `borderColor`: Adds a border to the button.

Button States

Consider the different states of a button and provide visual feedback for each:

Normal: The default appearance of the button.

Pressed: The appearance when the button is pressed.

Disabled: The appearance when the button is disabled.

Enhancing Interactions

You can enhance button interactions with:

Animations: Use the `Animated` API or other animation libraries to create subtle animations on press.

Haptic Feedback: Provide haptic feedback (vibrations) to confirm button presses.

Icons: Include icons within buttons to enhance visual communication.

Examples and Inspiration

Showcase examples of different button styles and interactions:

Call to action buttons: Use contrasting colors and clear labels to encourage user action.

Ghost buttons: Use transparent backgrounds and borders for a subtle look.

Floating action buttons: Circular buttons that stand out from the UI and trigger primary actions.

By mastering the art of button design and interaction, you can create a user-friendly and engaging experience in your React Native app. Well-designed buttons guide users, provide clear feedback, and enhance the overall usability of your app.

6.2 Modals and Overlays

(Creating focused user experiences with modal windows)

Modals and overlays are powerful tools for creating focused user experiences within your React Native app. They provide a way to temporarily interrupt the user's current flow and present important information, gather input, or guide them through a specific task.

What are Modals and Overlays?

Modals: Modals are UI elements that appear on top of the main content, typically as a centered window or dialog box. They require the user to interact with them before they can return to the underlying content.

Overlays: Overlays are similar to modals, but they can take up the entire screen or a portion of it. They often create a dimmed or blurred background to emphasize the overlayed content.

Use Cases for Modals and Overlays

Alerts and Notifications: Display important messages or notifications that require user acknowledgement.

Confirmation Dialogs: Confirm user actions before proceeding, such as deleting an item or making a purchase.

Forms and Input: Gather user input through forms or dialogs.

Progress Indicators: Display progress updates or loading states.

Tutorials and Guides: Guide users through features or onboarding processes.

Implementing Modals in React Native

React Native provides the `Modal` component for creating modal windows. You can control the visibility of the modal using a state variable and trigger its appearance based on user actions or events.

JavaScript

```javascript
import React, { useState } from 'react';

import { Modal, View, Text, Button, StyleSheet } from 'react-native';


const MyComponent = () => {

    const [modalVisible, setModalVisible] = useState(false);


  return (

    <View>

        <Button title="Open Modal" onPress={() => setModalVisible(true)} />


      <Modal

        animationType="slide"

        transparent={true}

        visible={modalVisible}

        onRequestClose={() => {

          setModalVisible(!modalVisible);

        }}

      >
```

```
      <View style={styles.centeredView}>
        <View style={styles.modalView}>
          <Text style={styles.modalText}>Hello from the Modal!</Text>
             <Button title="Close Modal" onPress={() => setModalVisible(false)} />
        </View>
      </View>
    </Modal>
  </View>
  );
};


const styles = StyleSheet.create({
  // ... styles for modal container and content
});
```

Customizing Modals

You can customize the appearance and behavior of modals using various props:

`animationType`: Controls the animation style (e.g., `slide`, `fade`).

`transparent`: Makes the modal background transparent.

`onRequestClose`: A function called when the user tries to close the modal (e.g., by pressing the back button).

Best Practices

Focus on the User's Goal: Design modals to help users achieve a specific goal or task.

Keep it Concise: Present information clearly and concisely. Avoid overwhelming users with too much content.

Provide Clear Actions: Offer clear and distinct actions, such as "Confirm" or "Cancel."

Accessibility: Ensure modals are accessible to users with disabilities (e.g., keyboard navigation, screen reader compatibility).

Examples and Inspiration

Showcase examples of effective modal usage in popular apps:

Image viewer modals in photo apps.

Confirmation dialogs for deleting items.

Onboarding modals with guided tutorials.

By mastering modals and overlays, you can create focused and engaging user experiences in your React Native app. These elements provide a powerful way to present important information, gather input, and guide users through specific tasks, enhancing the overall usability and effectiveness of your app.

6.3 Progress Indicators and Loaders

(Providing feedback during data fetching and processing)

In today's fast-paced digital world, users expect instant gratification. When your app needs time to fetch data, process information, or perform tasks, it's crucial to provide visual feedback to keep users informed and engaged. Progress indicators and loaders are essential tools for achieving this.

Why Use Progress Indicators and Loaders?

Transparency: They communicate to users that the app is actively working and hasn't frozen or crashed.

Managing Expectations: They provide an estimate of how long a process might take, reducing user anxiety and preventing them from abandoning the app.

Enhanced User Experience: They create a more polished and professional feel, showing that your app is responsive and well-designed.

Types of Progress Indicators

Activity Indicators (Spinners): These are indeterminate indicators that show that a process is ongoing without providing a specific completion time. They are ideal for tasks with unknown durations, such as loading data from a network.

Progress Bars: These are determinate indicators that display the progress of a task with a visual bar that fills up as the task progresses. They are suitable for tasks with known durations, such as file uploads or downloads.

Implementing Progress Indicators in React Native

React Native provides built-in components for both activity indicators and progress bars.

`ActivityIndicator`: Displays a circular spinner.

JavaScript

```
import { ActivityIndicator } from 'react-native';
```

```
<ActivityIndicator size="large" color="#0000ff" />
```

`ProgressBarAndroid` **(Android)** and `ProgressViewIOS` **(iOS):** Display platform-specific progress bars.

JavaScript

```
import { ProgressBarAndroid, ProgressViewIOS, Platform } from 'react-native';
```

```
{Platform.OS === 'android' ? (

    <ProgressBarAndroid styleAttr="Horizontal" progress={0.5} />

) : (

  <ProgressViewIOS progress={0.5} />

)}
```

Customizing Progress Indicators

You can customize the appearance of progress indicators using various props:

`size`: Controls the size of the indicator (e.g., `small`, `large`).

`color`: Sets the color of the indicator.

`style`: Applies custom styles to the indicator.

Best Practices

Provide Context: Accompany progress indicators with clear and concise text explaining what's happening.

Use Appropriate Indicators: Choose the right type of indicator based on the nature of the task (determinate or indeterminate).

Placement: Place indicators strategically within the UI to provide clear visual feedback.

Animation: Use subtle animations to make indicators more visually engaging.

Examples and Inspiration

Showcase examples of effective progress indicator usage in popular apps:

Loading spinners in web browsers.

Progress bars during file uploads or downloads.

Progress indicators in games or simulations.

By thoughtfully implementing progress indicators and loaders in your React Native app, you can enhance the user experience by providing clear feedback, managing expectations, and creating a more polished and professional feel.

Chapter 7

Animations for Delightful Interactions

7.1 The Animated API

(Understanding animation principles and techniques in React Native)

Animations breathe life into your app. They transform static interfaces into dynamic experiences, delighting users and enhancing usability. React Native's `Animated` API provides a powerful and flexible toolkit for creating a wide range of animations, from simple transitions to complex interactions.

Core Concepts

`Animated.Value`: This is the heart of the `Animated` API. It represents a value that can be animated over time. You can create `Animated.Value` instances for various properties like position, scale, opacity, and color.

Animation Drivers: These define how the animated value changes over time. Common drivers include:

`Animated.timing`: Animates a value over a specified duration with easing functions.

`Animated.spring`: Creates spring-like animations with bounciness and friction.

`Animated.decay`: Starts an animation that decays over time, like a ball losing momentum.

`Animated` **Components**: These are special components that can be animated using `Animated.Value` instances. Common examples include `Animated.View`, `Animated.Text`, and `Animated.Image`.

Interpolation: This allows you to map animated values to different ranges or outputs. For example, you can map an opacity value from 0 to 1 to a scale value from 0.5 to 1.

Basic Animation Example

Let's create a simple animation that fades a view in and out:

JavaScript

```
import React, { useRef, useEffect } from 'react';
import { Animated, View, StyleSheet } from 'react-native';


const FadeInView = (props) => {
    const fadeAnim = useRef(new Animated.Value(0)).current;


  useEffect(() => {
    Animated.timing(fadeAnim, {
      toValue: 1,
```

```
      duration:¹ 1000,
      useNativeDriver: true,
    }).start();
  }, [fadeAnim]);

  return (
      <Animated.View  style={{  ...props.style,
opacity: fadeAnim }}>
      {props.children}
    </Animated.View>²
  );
};


const App = () => {
  return (
    <View style={styles.container}>
      <FadeInView style={styles.fadingContainer}>
        <Text style={styles.fadingText}>Fading View!</Text>
      </FadeInView>
    </View>
```

```
  );
};


const styles = StyleSheet.create({
  container: {
    flex: 1,
    alignItems: 'center',
    justifyContent: 'center',
  },
  fadingContainer: {
    padding: 20,
    backgroundColor: 'powderblue',
  },
  fadingText: {
    fontSize:[3] 28,
    textAlign: 'center',
    margin: 10,
  },
});
```

Advanced Techniques

Combining Animations: You can combine multiple animations using `Animated.parallel` and `Animated.sequence` to create complex effects.

Gesture Integration: Integrate animations with gesture handlers to create interactive experiences.

Performance Optimization: Use `useNativeDriver: true` to offload animations to the native thread for smoother performance.

Examples and Inspiration

Showcase examples of how the `Animated` API can be used to create various animation effects:

Sliding menus.

Bouncing animations.

Loading indicators.

Animated transitions between screens.

By understanding the `Animated` API and its core principles, you can unlock a world of possibilities for creating delightful and engaging animations in your React Native app.

7.2 Creating Micro-interactions

(Adding subtle animations for feedback and engagement)

While grand, sweeping animations can be impressive, sometimes the most delightful and effective animations are the subtle ones. Micro-interactions are those small, almost invisible animations that provide feedback, guide the user, and add a touch of polish to your app.

What are Micro-interactions?

Micro-interactions are short, focused animations that occur in response to user actions or system events. They are designed to be subtle and unobtrusive, yet they play a crucial role in enhancing the user experience.

Benefits of Micro-interactions

Provide Feedback: They confirm user actions and provide immediate visual feedback, making the app feel more responsive.

Guide the User: They can subtly guide the user's attention, highlighting important elements or changes in the UI.

Enhance Engagement: They add a touch of delight and personality to the app, making it more engaging and enjoyable to use.

Communicate Status: They can visually communicate the status of a process or action, such as loading, success, or failure.

Examples of Micro-interactions

Button Animations: A button might subtly scale or change color when pressed.

Toggle Switches: A toggle switch might animate smoothly when switched on or off.

Loading Indicators: A loading spinner might have a subtle pulsing animation.

Notifications: A notification might slide in from the top of the screen with a gentle bounce.

Hover Effects: An element might subtly scale or change color when the user hovers over it.

Implementing Micro-interactions in React Native

You can implement micro-interactions using the `Animated` API or other animation libraries. The key is to keep the animations small, fast, and relevant to the user's action.

Example: Animated Button

JavaScript

```javascript
import React, { useRef } from 'react';

import { Animated, TouchableOpacity, Text, StyleSheet } from 'react-native';


const AnimatedButton = ({ title, onPress }) => {

  const scale = useRef(new Animated.Value(1)).current;


  const handlePressIn = () => {

    Animated.spring(scale, {

      toValue: 0.95,

      useNativeDriver: true,

    }).start();

  };


  const handlePressOut = () => {
```

```
    Animated.spring(scale, {
        toValue: 1,
        useNativeDriver: true,
    }).start();[1]
};


return (
    <TouchableOpacity
        onPressIn={handlePressIn}
        onPressOut={handlePressOut}
        onPress={onPress}
    >
        <Animated.View style={[styles.button, { transform: [{ scale }] }]}>
            <Text style={styles.buttonText}>{title}</Text>
        </Animated.View>
    </TouchableOpacity>
);
};
```

```
const styles = StyleSheet.create({
  // ... button styles
});
```

Best Practices

Subtlety is Key: Micro-interactions should be subtle and not distract from the main content.

Keep it Short: Animations should be quick and snappy.

Context is Important: Micro-interactions should be relevant to the user's action or the context of the UI.

Don't Overuse: Too many micro-interactions can be overwhelming and distracting.

By adding well-designed micro-interactions to your React Native app, you can enhance the user experience, making it more engaging, delightful, and user-friendly. These subtle animations provide valuable feedback, guide the user, and add a touch of polish that elevates your app's overall quality.

7.3 Advanced Animation Techniques

(Implementing complex animations and transitions)

While basic animations can add a touch of flair to your app, mastering advanced techniques allows you to create truly captivating and dynamic user experiences. React Native's `Animated` API, combined with creative thinking and a bit of code, can unlock a world of possibilities for complex animations and transitions.

1. Orchestrating Animations with `Animated.parallel` and `Animated.sequence`

`Animated.parallel`: Run multiple animations simultaneously. This is useful for creating effects where different properties animate at the same time, such as fading in an element while also scaling it up.

JavaScript

```javascript
Animated.parallel([
  Animated.timing(opacity, { toValue: 1 }),
  Animated.spring(scale, { toValue: 1.2 })
]).start();
```

`Animated.sequence`: Run animations one after another in a specific order. This is great for creating staged animations, like sliding an element in, then fading it in.

JavaScript

```javascript
Animated.sequence([
  Animated.timing(position, { toValue: 0 }),
  Animated.timing(opacity, { toValue: 1 })
]).start();
```

2. Gesture-Driven Animations

Combine the `Animated` API with gesture handlers like `PanResponder` or `react-native-gesture-handler` to create interactive animations that respond to user touch input.

Example: Create a draggable element that follows the user's finger, or a card that can be swiped away.

This technique allows for dynamic and engaging interactions, giving users a sense of direct manipulation and control.

3. Shared Element Transitions

Create seamless transitions between screens where elements appear to move smoothly from one screen to another. This creates a sense of visual continuity and enhances the user's mental model of the app's navigation.

Libraries: `react-native-shared-element` and `react-navigation-shared-element` can help implement these transitions.

Example: An image in a list smoothly expands to become the hero image on a detail screen.

4. Animated Values as Styles

Use `Animated.Value` instances directly within your component's styles to create dynamic and responsive animations.

Example: Change the background color of a view based on scroll position, or create a progress bar that animates as data loads.

This technique allows for tight integration between animations and your UI, creating a cohesive and visually appealing experience.

5. Interpolation for Advanced Mapping

Use `Animated.interpolate` to map animated values to different ranges, outputs, or even other animated values.

Example: Map a scroll position to the rotation of an element, or create a color animation that changes hue as a value progresses.

Interpolation unlocks a wide range of creative possibilities for complex and nuanced animations.

Best Practices

Performance: Be mindful of performance, especially with complex animations. Use `useNativeDriver` where possible and optimize your code to avoid unnecessary re-renders.

User Experience: Animations should enhance the user experience, not distract from it. Keep animations subtle, purposeful, and relevant to the user's actions.

Accessibility: Consider users with motion sensitivities or visual impairments. Provide options to disable or reduce animations if needed.

By mastering these advanced animation techniques, you can elevate your React Native app to a new level of polish and engagement. Complex animations and transitions can delight users, enhance navigation, and create a truly memorable experience.

Chapter 8

Platform-Specific Styling and Adaptations

8.1 Detecting Platform Differences

(Identifying iOS and Android design conventions)

While React Native's "learn once, write anywhere" philosophy is powerful, it's important to recognize that iOS and Android have distinct design conventions and user expectations. Crafting truly elegant UIs often requires adapting your app to these platform-specific nuances.

Why Platform-Specific Design Matters

User Expectations: Users are accustomed to certain design patterns and interactions on their respective platforms. Adhering to these conventions makes your app feel familiar and intuitive.

Visual Harmony: Platform-specific design ensures your app integrates seamlessly with the overall look and feel of the operating system.

Brand Consistency: While adapting to platform conventions, you can still maintain your brand identity through consistent use of colors, typography, and visual language.

Key Differences to Consider

Navigation:

iOS: Typically uses a tab bar at the bottom for primary navigation and a back button in the top left corner.

Android: Often uses a tab bar at the top or a navigation drawer for primary navigation and a system-wide back button.

Buttons:

iOS: Buttons tend to have rounded corners and subtle shadows.

Android: Buttons often have sharp corners and use Material Design's elevation system for shadows.

Typography:

iOS: Favors the San Francisco font family.

Android: Uses the Roboto font family.

Icons:

iOS: Icons are typically filled and have a more realistic style.

Android: Icons tend to be outlined and have a more geometric style.

Spacing and Layout:

iOS: Emphasizes larger spacing and margins.

Android: Uses denser spacing and layout.

Detecting the Platform in React Native

React Native provides the `Platform` module for detecting the current platform. You can use `Platform.OS` to conditionally render different components or styles based on whether the app is running on iOS or Android.

JavaScript

```
import { Platform, StyleSheet } from 'react-native';
```

```
const styles = StyleSheet.create({
  container: {
    padding: Platform.OS === 'ios' ? 20 : 10,
  },
});
```

Best Practices

Follow Platform Guidelines: Refer to Apple's Human Interface Guidelines and Google's Material Design guidelines for detailed design conventions.

Prioritize Consistency: Maintain consistency within your app, even when adapting to platform differences.

Test on Both Platforms: Thoroughly test your app on both iOS and Android devices to ensure it looks and functions correctly.

Tools and Resources

Platform-Specific Component Libraries: Consider using libraries like `react-native-elements` or `native-base` that offer pre-styled components adapted to each platform.

Design Systems: Create a design system that defines platform-specific variations of your UI components.

By understanding and adapting to platform differences, you can create a React Native app that feels truly native on both iOS and Android. This attention to detail enhances the user experience, making your app more intuitive, visually harmonious, and consistent with user expectations.

8.2 Conditional Rendering for Platform-Specific UI

(Adapting your UI for each platform)

While React Native strives for cross-platform compatibility, sometimes you need to tailor your UI to match specific design conventions or utilize platform-exclusive features. Conditional rendering allows you to dynamically adjust your UI based on the platform the app is running on, creating a more native and intuitive experience for users.

The Power of `Platform`

React Native's `Platform` module is your key to conditional rendering. It provides a simple API for detecting the current platform and making decisions based on it.

`Platform.OS`: This property returns either `'ios'` or `'android'`, allowing you to identify the platform.

Conditional Rendering Techniques

Ternary Operator: This concise operator lets you render different components or elements based on a condition.

JavaScript

```
import { Platform, View, Text } from 'react-native';
```

```
<View>
    {Platform.OS === 'ios' ? <Text>This is iOS</Text> : <Text>This is Android</Text>}
```

```
</View>
```

`Platform.select`: This method provides a more structured way to handle platform-specific rendering, especially for multiple platforms or complex conditions.

JavaScript

```
import { Platform, StyleSheet } from 'react-native';

const styles = StyleSheet.create({
  container: {
    padding: Platform.select({
      ios: 20,
      android: 10,
      default: 15, // For other platforms
    }),
  },
});
```

Platform-Specific Files: For more extensive platform-specific code, you can create separate files with `.ios.js` and `.android.js` extensions. React Native will automatically load the appropriate file based on the platform.

JavaScript

```javascript
// MyComponent.ios.js
// ... iOS-specific code


// MyComponent.android.js
// ... Android-specific code
```

Common Use Cases

Navigation: Render different navigation components (tab bars, navigation drawers) based on platform conventions.

Styling: Apply platform-specific styles for margins, padding, fonts, and shadows.

UI Elements: Use platform-specific UI elements like segmented controls (iOS) or switches (Android).

Platform-Exclusive Features: Access features that are only available on one platform, such as haptic feedback or certain sensors.

Best Practices

Balance Consistency and Customization: Strive for a consistent user experience across platforms while still adapting to platform-specific conventions.

Keep Code Maintainable: Organize your code to avoid excessive branching and ensure maintainability.

Test Thoroughly: Test your app on both iOS and Android to ensure it renders and functions correctly on each platform.

By mastering conditional rendering techniques, you can create a React Native app that feels truly native on both iOS and Android. This attention to detail enhances the user experience, making your app more intuitive, visually harmonious, and consistent with user expectations.

8.3 Using Native Modules for Platform-Specific Features

(Accessing native UI elements)

While React Native provides a comprehensive set of built-in components, there might be times when you need to access platform-specific UI elements or features that aren't available in the core framework. This is where Native Modules come into play, bridging the gap between your JavaScript code and the native capabilities of iOS and Android.

What are Native Modules?

Native Modules are essentially pieces of code written in the native languages of each platform (Java/Kotlin for Android and Objective-C/Swift for iOS) that expose native functionalities to your React Native JavaScript code. They act as a bridge, allowing you to tap into the full power of the underlying platform.

Why Use Native Modules?

Access Platform-Specific UI: Implement UI elements that are unique to each platform, such as date pickers, activity views, or sharing dialogs.

Utilize Native Features: Access device-specific features like the camera, GPS, Bluetooth, or sensors.

Integrate with Native Libraries: Leverage existing native libraries or SDKs to add functionalities to your app.

Performance Optimization: Offload computationally intensive tasks to native code for improved performance.

Creating and Using Native Modules

Creating a Native Module involves writing native code for each platform and exposing it to React Native using a specific bridge interface. This process requires knowledge of native mobile development.

Once a Native Module is created, you can access it in your JavaScript code using the `NativeModules` object.

JavaScript

```
import { NativeModules } from 'react-native';


const MyNativeModule = NativeModules.MyModule;


MyNativeModule.myNativeFunction(arg1,          arg2,
(result) => {

   // Handle the result from the native function
```

```
});
```

Example: Accessing a Native UI Element

Let's say you want to use a native date picker that looks and behaves consistently with the user's platform. You could create a Native Module that exposes the native date picker functionality to your React Native code.

Best Practices

Minimize Native Code: Use Native Modules only when necessary. Strive to use React Native components and APIs whenever possible.

Follow Platform Conventions: When implementing platform-specific UI, adhere to the design guidelines of each platform to ensure a consistent and intuitive user experience.

Error Handling: Implement robust error handling in both your native and JavaScript code to gracefully handle potential issues.

Documentation: Clearly document your Native Modules to make them easy to understand and use.

Tools and Resources

React Native Documentation: Refer to the official React Native documentation for detailed guides on creating and using Native Modules.

Community Libraries: Explore community-contributed libraries that offer pre-built Native Modules for common functionalities.

By leveraging Native Modules, you can extend the capabilities of your React Native app and create truly native experiences. This powerful technique allows you to access platform-specific UI elements, utilize native features, and integrate with existing native libraries, enhancing the functionality and performance of your app.

Chapter 9

Design Systems and Component Libraries

9.1 Building Reusable UI Components

(Creating a library of consistent and maintainable components)

Imagine building a house where you have to craft every door, window, and cabinet from scratch each time. It would be incredibly time-consuming and inefficient. The same applies to UI development. Building reusable UI components is essential for creating maintainable, scalable, and consistent React Native applications.

Why Reusable Components?

Efficiency: Write code once and reuse it throughout your app, saving time and effort.

Consistency: Maintain a unified look and feel across your app, ensuring a cohesive user experience.

Maintainability: Updates and bug fixes become easier as changes only need to be made in one place.

Scalability: Easily add new features or screens without rewriting existing components.

Collaboration: Reusable components promote collaboration among developers, as they can share and reuse each other's work.

Identifying Reusable Candidates

Look for UI elements that appear repeatedly in your app, such as:

Buttons: Primary, secondary, icon buttons, etc.

Inputs: Text fields, password inputs, dropdowns.

Cards: Product cards, user profiles, news items.

Headers: Navigation bars, section headers.

Modals: Dialogs, alerts, confirmation boxes.

Creating Reusable Components

Identify Props: Determine the properties that will allow your component to be customized for different use cases. For example, a button component might have props for `title`, `onPress`, `color`, and `size`.

Implement Logic: Encapsulate the component's logic and behavior within its own function or class.

Style with Flexibility: Use stylesheets or styling libraries to create flexible and adaptable styles. Consider using theme variables to support different themes.

Test Thoroughly: Write unit tests to ensure your component behaves as expected in various scenarios.

Example: Reusable Button Component

JavaScript

```
import React from 'react';

import { TouchableOpacity, Text, StyleSheet } from 'react-native';
```

```
const MyButton = ({ title, onPress, color, size }) => {
  return (
    <TouchableOpacity style={[styles.button, { backgroundColor: color, padding: size }]} onPress={onPress}>
      <Text style={styles.buttonText}>{title}</Text>
    </TouchableOpacity>
  );
};


const styles = StyleSheet.create({
  button: {
    borderRadius:[1] 5,
    alignItems: 'center',
    justifyContent: 'center',
  },
  buttonText:[2] {
    color: '#fff',
    fontSize: 16,
  },
```

```
});
```

```
export default MyButton;
```

Organizing Your Component Library

Create a dedicated folder for your reusable components. Organize them into categories or modules for easy access and maintainability.

Best Practices

Keep Components Small and Focused: Each component should have a single responsibility.

Use Composition: Combine smaller components to create more complex ones.

Document Clearly: Document your components with clear descriptions and usage examples.

Version Control: Use a version control system like Git to track changes and collaborate effectively.

By building a library of reusable UI components, you can significantly improve the efficiency, consistency, and maintainability of your React Native app. This approach promotes a more modular and scalable architecture, allowing you to focus on building great features instead of reinventing the wheel.

9.2 Implementing a Design System

(Defining style guidelines and component specifications)

A design system is more than just a collection of reusable components. It's a comprehensive set of guidelines, principles, and specifications that govern the design and development of your app's UI. Think of it as a single source of truth that ensures consistency, efficiency, and maintainability across your entire project.

Key Elements of a Design System

Style Guidelines:

Color Palette: Define a core set of colors with specific usage guidelines (primary, secondary, accent, error, etc.). Include color values in different formats (hex, RGB, HSL) and accessibility considerations (contrast ratios).

Typography: Specify font families, sizes, weights, and line heights for different text elements (headings, body text, labels, etc.). Define rules for text alignment, spacing, and capitalization.

Spacing: Establish a spacing system using a consistent unit (e.g., 8pt grid) to create visual rhythm and harmony. Define spacing values for margins, padding, and gaps between elements.

Imagery: Provide guidelines for image usage, including aspect ratios, image quality, and accessibility considerations (alt text).

Iconography: Define a consistent style for icons, including size, color, and usage guidelines.

Component Specifications:

Purpose and Usage: Clearly define the purpose and intended usage of each component.

Props and Variations: Document the available props for customization and any variations of the component (e.g., different sizes, states, or styles).

Accessibility: Specify accessibility considerations for each component, such as keyboard navigation, screen reader compatibility, and ARIA attributes.

Code Examples: Provide clear code examples demonstrating how to use each component.

Design Principles:

Brand Identity: Articulate the core values and personality of your brand and how they should be reflected in the UI.

User Experience: Define principles for user-centered design, such as usability, accessibility, and consistency.

Implementation Guidelines: Provide guidance on how to implement the design system in code, including naming conventions, file structure, and coding standards.

Tools and Resources

Documentation Platforms: Use tools like Zeroheight, Storybook, or Notion to create a centralized hub for your design system documentation.

Component Libraries: Leverage existing component libraries like Material UI or React Native Elements as a foundation for your design system.

Design Tools: Use design tools like Figma or Sketch to create visual representations of your components and style guidelines.

Benefits of a Design System

Improved Consistency: Ensures a unified look and feel across your app.

Increased Efficiency: Reduces design and development time by reusing components and styles.

Enhanced Maintainability: Makes it easier to update and maintain your app's UI.

Improved Collaboration: Facilitates communication and collaboration between designers and developers.

Scalability: Supports the growth and evolution of your app over time.

By implementing a comprehensive design system, you can create a more cohesive, efficient, and maintainable React Native app. It serves as a valuable resource for your team, guiding design decisions, promoting consistency, and ensuring a high-quality user experience.

9.3 Utilizing Popular UI Libraries

(Exploring and integrating existing component libraries)

While building your own reusable components and design system is a powerful approach, you don't always have to start from scratch. React Native boasts a thriving ecosystem of popular UI libraries that offer pre-built components, styles, and design systems, allowing you to accelerate development and leverage the expertise of the community.

Benefits of Using UI Libraries

Faster Development: Get a head start on your project by using ready-made components, saving valuable time and effort.

Consistent Design: Benefit from a cohesive design language and style guide, ensuring a polished and professional look and feel.

Community Support: Leverage the knowledge and experience of a large community of developers, with readily available documentation, tutorials, and support.

Accessibility: Many UI libraries prioritize accessibility, providing components that adhere to accessibility standards and best practices.

Cross-Platform Compatibility: Most UI libraries are designed to work seamlessly on both iOS and Android, reducing platform-specific styling issues.

Popular React Native UI Libraries

React Native Elements: A highly customizable and widely used library offering a comprehensive set of components, including buttons, inputs, icons, badges, and more.

NativeBase: A popular choice for building cross-platform apps with a focus on Material Design. It provides a wide range of components and theme support.

React Native Paper: A Material Design-inspired library from Callstack that offers a clean and modern look and feel. It features components like buttons, cards, dialogs, and bottom navigation.

Lottie for React Native: A library for adding delightful animations to your app using Lottie files created in Adobe After Effects.

React Native Vector Icons: A library that provides a vast collection of popular icon sets, including FontAwesome, Material Icons, and Ionicons.

Integrating UI Libraries

Installation: Install the library using npm or yarn.

Bash

```
npm install react-native-elements
```

Import Components: Import the components you need from the library.

JavaScript

```
import { Button, Input } from 'react-native-elements';
```

Customization: Most UI libraries offer theming and customization options to adapt the components to your brand's visual style.

Best Practices

Choose the Right Library: Select a library that aligns with your project's design goals, component needs, and development style.

Read the Documentation: Familiarize yourself with the library's documentation to understand its components, APIs, and customization options.

Stay Updated: Keep the library up-to-date to benefit from bug fixes, performance improvements, and new features.

Contribute Back: Consider contributing to the library's development by reporting issues, submitting pull requests, or sharing your experiences.

By utilizing popular UI libraries, you can accelerate your React Native development, leverage community expertise, and create beautiful and consistent user interfaces. These libraries provide valuable tools and resources that empower you to focus on building unique features and delivering exceptional user experiences.

Chapter 10

Accessibility and Inclusive Design

10.1 Understanding Accessibility Principles

(Designing for users with disabilities)

Accessibility is not just a good practice, it's a moral imperative. Designing with accessibility in mind ensures that your app can be used by everyone, regardless of their abilities. This includes people with visual, auditory, motor, or cognitive disabilities. In this section, we'll explore the core principles of accessibility and how they apply to React Native development.

The POUR Principles of Accessibility

The Web Content Accessibility Guidelines (WCAG) outline four main principles that make content accessible to people with disabilities:

Perceivable: Users must be able to perceive the information being presented. This means providing text alternatives for images, captions for videos, and ensuring sufficient color contrast.

Operable: Users must be able to operate the interface. This means making all functionality available via keyboard, providing clear navigation, and avoiding time limits that could create barriers.

Understandable: Users must be able to understand the information and how to use the interface. This means using clear and simple language, consistent navigation patterns, and providing help and documentation.

Robust: Content must be robust enough that it can be interpreted reliably by a wide variety of user agents, including assistive technologies. This means using semantic HTML, providing alternative input methods, and ensuring compatibility with screen readers.

Applying Accessibility Principles in React Native

Text Alternatives: Use the `accessibilityLabel` prop to provide descriptive labels for images and other non-textual elements.

Color Contrast: Ensure sufficient contrast between text and background colors using tools like WebAIM's Color Contrast Checker.

Keyboard Navigation: Make sure all interactive elements can be accessed and operated using the keyboard. Use the `accessible` and `accessibilityRole` props to define the element's role and behavior.

Screen Reader Compatibility: Use semantic HTML elements and ARIA attributes to provide meaningful information to screen readers.

Touch Target Size: Ensure touch targets are large enough and spaced sufficiently apart to be easily tapped by users with motor impairments.

Time Limits: Avoid time limits or provide mechanisms to extend them, allowing users with cognitive disabilities or slower reading speeds to complete tasks.

Animations and Transitions: Provide options to disable or reduce animations for users with motion sensitivities or vestibular disorders.

Testing for Accessibility

Manual Testing: Use a keyboard to navigate your app and a screen reader to experience it from the perspective of a visually impaired user.

Automated Testing: Use accessibility testing tools like `eslint-plugin-jsx-a11y` to identify potential accessibility issues in your code.

User Testing: Conduct user testing with people with disabilities to gather feedback and identify areas for improvement.

Beyond Compliance

Accessibility is not just about meeting minimum requirements. It's about creating an inclusive and welcoming experience for all users. Consider going beyond basic compliance by:

Providing multiple input methods: Support voice control, gestures, and other input methods.

Offering customizable settings: Allow users to adjust font sizes, colors, and other visual settings to meet their individual needs.

Using inclusive language: Use language that is respectful and inclusive of all users.

By understanding and applying accessibility principles in your React Native app, you can create a truly inclusive experience that welcomes everyone, regardless of their abilities. This not only benefits users with disabilities but also improves the overall usability and quality of your app for all users.

10.2 Implementing Accessibility Features

(Using screen readers, keyboard navigation, and ARIA attributes)

Making your React Native app truly accessible involves going beyond just understanding the principles. It requires actively implementing features that cater to users with various disabilities. Let's delve into the practical aspects of implementing accessibility features, focusing on screen readers, keyboard navigation, and ARIA attributes.

1. Screen Readers: Providing Auditory Access

Screen readers are assistive technologies that read aloud the content of the screen, allowing visually impaired users to interact with the app. To ensure your app works seamlessly with screen readers:

`accessibilityLabel`: Use this prop to provide concise and descriptive labels for all interactive elements, including buttons, images, and text inputs. This label is what the screen reader will announce to the user.

JavaScript

```
<TouchableOpacity accessibilityLabel="Submit the form">
  <Text>Submit</Text>
</TouchableOpacity>
```

`accessibilityHint`: Provide additional context or instructions for interactive elements using this prop. This hint helps users understand the purpose and functionality of the element.

JavaScript

```
<Button
  title="Delete"
  accessibilityHint="This will permanently delete the item"
```

```
/>
```

`accessibilityRole`: Define the semantic role of an element using this prop. This helps screen readers understand the purpose of the element and provide appropriate feedback to the user.

JavaScript

```
<View accessibilityRole="header">
  {/* Header content */}
</View>
```

2. Keyboard Navigation: Enabling Accessibility without a Mouse

Many users rely on keyboard navigation to interact with apps. To ensure your app is fully navigable using only the keyboard:

`accessible`: Set this prop to `true` for all interactive elements to make them focusable using the Tab key.

`onFocus` **and** `onBlur`: Use these props to provide visual feedback when an element gains or loses focus. This helps users understand where they are in the navigation flow.

Logical Tab Order: Ensure the tab order flows logically through the screen, following a natural reading order.

3. ARIA Attributes: Enhancing Semantic Information

ARIA (Accessible Rich Internet Applications) attributes provide additional semantic information to assistive technologies, enhancing the accessibility of your app.

`aria-label`: Similar to `accessibilityLabel`, this attribute provides a label for elements that don't have visible labels.

`aria-labelledby`: Associate an element with another element that provides its label.

`aria-describedby`: Associate an element with another element that provides a description or instructions.

`aria-hidden`: Hide elements from screen readers if they are purely visual or redundant.

`aria-expanded`, `aria-checked`, `aria-selected`: Communicate the state of interactive elements like accordions, checkboxes, and radio buttons.

Testing and Iteration

Use a Screen Reader: Test your app with a screen reader like VoiceOver (iOS) or TalkBack (Android) to experience it from the perspective of a visually impaired user.

Keyboard-Only Navigation: Navigate your app using only the Tab key and arrow keys to ensure all interactive elements are accessible.

Accessibility Audits: Use accessibility auditing tools to identify potential issues and ensure your app meets accessibility standards.

By actively implementing these accessibility features in your React Native app, you can create a more inclusive and user-friendly experience for everyone. This not only benefits users with disabilities but also enhances the overall usability and quality of your app for all users.

10.3 Testing for Accessibility

(Ensuring your app is usable by everyone)

Building an accessible app is an ongoing process. It's not enough to just implement accessibility features; you need to rigorously test your app to ensure it truly works for everyone. This involves putting yourself in the shoes of users with different disabilities and experiencing your app from their perspective.

1. Manual Testing

Keyboard Navigation: Put away your mouse or trackpad and try navigating your app using only the Tab key, arrow keys, and Enter/Return key. Can you access all interactive elements? Does the tab order flow logically? Are there any keyboard traps?

Screen Reader Testing: Use a screen reader like VoiceOver (iOS) or TalkBack (Android) to experience your app through auditory feedback. Is the content being read clearly and in a logical order? Are interactive elements properly labeled and described? Are there any confusing or redundant elements?

Visual Impairment Simulation: Use your device's accessibility settings to simulate different types of visual impairments, such as color blindness, low vision, or no vision. Can you still use the app effectively? Are colors and contrasts sufficient? Are fonts legible?

Motor Impairment Simulation: Try using your app with one hand or with a stylus to simulate limited dexterity. Are touch targets large enough and spaced appropriately? Can you easily interact with all elements?

2. Automated Testing

Accessibility Auditing Tools: Use tools like `eslint-plugin-jsx-a11y` to automatically scan your code for potential accessibility issues. These tools can identify missing labels, insufficient color contrast, and other common problems.

Unit and Integration Tests: Include accessibility checks in your unit and integration tests to ensure that your components and features remain accessible as you make changes to your code.

3. User Testing with People with Disabilities

Recruit Diverse Participants: Involve people with a variety of disabilities in your user testing sessions. This will provide valuable insights into how different users experience your app.

Observe and Gather Feedback: Observe how users interact with your app and gather their feedback on any challenges they encounter.

Iterate and Improve: Use the feedback from user testing to identify areas for improvement and make your app more accessible.

Best Practices

Test Early and Often: Integrate accessibility testing throughout your development process, not just at the end.

Test on Real Devices: Test on a variety of real devices with different screen sizes, resolutions, and operating system versions.

Document Your Findings: Keep a record of your accessibility testing results and any identified issues.

Prioritize Accessibility: Make accessibility a priority throughout your development process.

By implementing a comprehensive accessibility testing strategy, you can ensure that your React Native app is usable by everyone, regardless of their abilities. This not only creates a more inclusive experience but also improves the overall usability and quality of your app for all users.